MIDORI
Brilliant Violinist

MIDORI
Brilliant Violinist

By Charnan Simon

CHILDRENS PRESS ®
CHICAGO

To Jessica, another fine
young violinist and friend

PHOTO CREDITS

©Brent Petersen—Cover
AP/Wide World—16
Aspen Music Festival/ © Charles Abbott—3, 25, 29,
    30, 31
© Marianne Barcellona—1, 2
Courtesy of the Barbican Centre Press Office—22
Courtesy of ICM Artists/Satoru Ishikawa—32
Courtesy of The Juilliard School—© Peter Schaaf, 12;
    Henry Grossman, 13
Courtesy of the London Symphony Orchestra/
    Malcolm Crowthers—27
© Don Pollard—24
Courtesy of Professional Children's School—15, 17
© Walter H. Scott—5, 6, 7, 9, 18, 19, 20, 26, 28
SuperStock, International—10, 14, 23

DESIGN AND ELECTRONIC COMPOSITION: Biner Design

Library of Congress Cataloging-in-Publication Data

Simon, Charnan.
    Midori / by Charnan Simon.
    p. cm. — (Picture story biography)
    Summary: A brief biography of Japanese-born violinist
Midori, who amazed the music world with her talent from
an early age.
    ISBN 0-516-04187-8
    1. Midori, 1971–   —Juvenile literature. 2. Violinists—
Biography—Juvenile literature. [1. Midori, 1971–   . 2.
Violinists.] I. Title. II. Series: Picture-story biographies.

ML3930.M62S5 1993   92-40674
787.2'092—dc20   CIP
[B]   MN AC

THE CROWD at Tanglewood Music
Festival was happy. Sitting under the
stars on a hot summer night, they were
enjoying the music of the Boston
Symphony Orchestra. Led by the
famous conductor Leonard Bernstein,
the orchestra was playing Bernstein's
own composition—"Serenade for
Violin and String Orchestra."

Midori in her Tanglewood debut

At the center of the huge concert stage stood a tiny figure—the soloist. She was a Japanese-born violinist named Midori. Just fourteen years old, Midori was a student at the Juilliard School in New York City. But she was playing with all the skill and artistry of a grown-up.

All went well through the first four movements of the Serenade. Then, suddenly, a string snapped on Midori's violin. Unable to play without this E-string, Midori borrowed a violin from a member of the orchestra. A few minutes later, the E-string on *that* violin snapped, too. Midori had to borrow yet another violin.

After a string breaks, Midori borrows another violin.

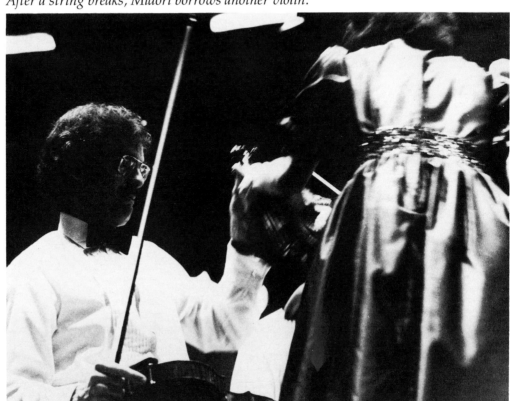

The young musician's predicament might have rattled a much more experienced performer. Twice, Midori's concentration had been broken. Twice, she had to stop playing to borrow a violin. To make things worse, each of the borrowed instruments was larger than her own specially made violin. Surely, everyone would have understood if the young violinist had seemed upset or made mistakes.

But Midori was unruffled. She finished playing the difficult serenade flawlessly, as if nothing out of the ordinary had happened. When the music ended, the audience leaped to their feet, cheering. Leonard Bernstein and the entire orchestra joined the audience in giving Midori a standing ovation. Here was a true musician!

After her performance at Tanglewood on July 26, 1986, Midori

When she finished her breathtaking performance, the audience, orchestra, and conductor (Leonard Bernstein) all gave Midori a standing ovation.

was famous. Front-page headlines in *The New York Times* announced: "Girl, 14, Conquers Tanglewood with 3 Violins!" Only Midori remained unfazed. "What else could I do?" she asked after the concert. "My strings broke, and I didn't want to stop the music."

Midori has never wanted to stop the music. She was born Mi Dori Goto on October 25, 1971, in Osaka, Japan. Her mother, Setsu Goto, was a well-known violinist. Setsu often took her young daughter with her to rehearsals, where Midori napped while her mother practiced.

Osaka, Japan, where Midori was born

One day, when Midori was just two years old, her mother heard her humming. Setsu Goto was astonished. The toddler was humming a difficult Bach concerto—music that Setsu had been rehearsing two days earlier. It was time for Midori to begin music lessons!

Midori was given her own violin on her third birthday. It was tiny, just large enough for her fingers to reach the strings. Every day, Setsu gave Midori a music lesson. Then Midori practiced in the kitchen while her mother made dinner.

By the time she was eight, Midori's talent was impressing many people. A family friend convinced Setsu to make a tape recording of Midori's favorite pieces. The tape was sent to Dorothy DeLay, a famous violin teacher at the Juilliard School of Music in New York.

Dorothy DeLay

Dorothy DeLay called Midori's playing "absolutely extraordinary." She immediately invited the young Japanese violinist to attend the Aspen Summer Music Festival in Colorado.

Midori and her mother traveled to the United States in the summer of 1981. Not yet ten years old, Midori amazed everyone who heard her play at the Aspen Festival. The world-famous violinist Pinchas Zukerman described her performance as a "miracle." And, best of all, Dorothy DeLay accepted Midori as her pupil at the Juilliard School.

By the fall of 1982, Midori and her mother had settled into a small studio apartment in New York City. It was hard to leave their home and friends in

The Juilliard School in New York City, where Midori studied music

Osaka, but New York offered more opportunities for Midori and her music.

Eleven-year-old Midori threw herself into her new life. She worked hard to improve her English and made friends with her American classmates. She learned what it was like to take violin lessons from someone other than her mother. She adjusted to the bewildering sights and sounds of bustling New York. "It was very

Midori grew to love the excitement of New York City.

Midori and classmates at the Professional Children's School, where she took academic classes while attending Juilliard for music

difficult," she admits. "It was the first time I went to a music school, the first time I had a teacher. Also, I had never been around so many kids before!"

And it was an exciting time. Shortly after she moved to New York, the famous conductor Zubin Mehta heard

Zubin Mehta, conductor of the New York Philharmonic, invited Midori to play at the 1982 New Year's Eve concert.

Midori play. He was so impressed that he invited her to perform with the New York Philharmonic Orchestra at its 1982 New Year's Eve concert. Midori received a standing ovation that night—and many invitations to play at other concerts around the world.

Now Midori had to juggle school,
music lessons, daily practice sessions,
and a growing number of performances.
At first, she played at only a few
concerts every year. Midori had much
to learn about life as a performing artist.
She had to learn the simple things, such
as the proper way to walk on and off a

*Even as a little
girl, Midori had
to practice for
many hours a day.*

stage. She also had to learn the complicated things, like how to play with different orchestras led by different conductors on different stages. She had to travel hundreds of miles and then play her violin the very next day. It was hard work for a young girl, but Midori loved it.

"My happiest times are spent playing the violin," she explains. "I just

Midori onstage

*One of Midori's many performances included a
1988 birthday tribute to Leonard Bernstein; the
conductor is Seiji Ozawa.*

love the feeling of standing on a stage;
it's the place I feel safest. And when
I'm playing with an orchestra, it's
really a magical moment, because then
it's a hundred of us joined in
producing one thing—music."

At a party, the great conductor Leonard Bernstein shows that he is a Midori fan.

After Midori's triumph at Tanglewood in 1986, she received even more invitations to perform. Finally, in 1987, when she was not yet sixteen years old, Midori left Juilliard. From now on, she would be a full-time professional violinist.

Not everyone agreed with Midori's decision. Some people felt it was too soon for her to stop taking music lessons. They said Midori still needed a teacher to guide her. They said that playing concerts so often would be too hard on such a young girl.

But Midori had always worked hard to get what she wanted. She would continue her regular classes at the Professional Children's School. She would take her schoolwork with her when she traveled to concerts. But she no longer felt she needed violin lessons. She wanted to perform!

And so she has. Since 1987, Midori has appeared on stages all around the world. She has met and played with some of the world's greatest musicians. Many times, she has been the youngest person onstage, but her performances have always been outstanding.

Midori has performed as many as ninety concerts in one year, but she prefers to play only about seventy. That is still more than one performance a week! "This way, I have time to practice and be in the best shape," she says. "I need some time off—and away from the violin—to think about the piece."

Midori has performed with the world's greatest orchestras, such as the London Symphony Orchestra.

Midori has also performed at world-famous Carnegie Hall in New York City.

Besides performing, Midori likes to record her favorite pieces on albums, tapes, and CDs. She made her first recording in 1986, when she was only fourteen years old. She has also played at the White House and made many television appearances—including one on the 1992 Winter Olympic Games telecast.

New York Governor Mario Cuomo presents Midori with an award in 1991.

Midori has received many awards for her work. In 1991, she was given New York State's Asian American Heritage Month Award. And though Midori now considers herself a New Yorker, she never forgets her Japanese heritage. She makes concert tours in Japan and says, "I like Japan, and I like coming back." Japan likes Midori, too.

She was given Japan's Crystal Award for her contribution to the arts, and in 1988, the Japanese government named her Best Artist of the Year.

People like Midori, who show extraordinary talent as children, are often called "prodigies." Sometimes these highly talented children grow up

Midori in rehearsal

to be equally talented adults. But sometimes their brilliance seems to fade away. Some people worried that Midori would "burn out" as she grew up.

Fortunately, this has not happened. Now a young adult, Midori is still growing as a musician. Critics still describe her performances as "brilliant," "exquisite," and "breathtaking."

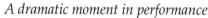
A dramatic moment in performance

Midori's childhood has been anything but ordinary, with friends like the famous conductor Michael Tilson Thomas!

Midori herself is more modest. "I don't know what I'd call myself, but I don't really consider myself a prodigy. I think a lot about music, but it keeps changing because I'm still growing. I go to concerts, opera, ballet, and museums; I adore reading. I never want to finish studying or growing."

When Midori was a teenager, she sometimes wondered what it would be like to have a different career. She considered going to college. She thought she would like to study French or history, or maybe become an archeologist.

But nothing could ever really compete with her music. "The longest I have ever been away from my violin is a day, and I missed it terribly," she told one interviewer. "It's hard to think of anything that brings me such joy as my work."

Midori performs at the Aspen Music Festival

Midori prepares to thrill yet another audience.

Practicing, performing, and traveling leave Midori very little spare time, but she loves to read and shop. She enjoys cooking even though she doesn't like to eat much—except dessert. "That's the only time my mom forces me to do anything," she admits. "She tells me to eat!"

Midori considers herself lucky to have a mother who has always

Midori in a solo recital

supported her interest in music. She knows that not all children are so fortunate. So, to help make music available to every child, Midori has set up a foundation. The Midori Foundation hopes to offer lecture-demonstrations, produce music videos, and establish musician-in-residence programs in schools around the world. As Midori says, "Music should be an enjoyable and enriching experience that can enhance a child's life."

Certainly music has enriched Midori's life. Those who know her are not surprised that she wants to share her joy in music with others. "I love playing," she says simply. "It isn't like there's me and then there's the violin. The violin is me. I love it so much that I want to share it with other people."

MIDORI

1971   October 25—Born in Osaka, Japan

1981   Traveled to United States for Aspen Festival

1982   Moved to New York City with her mother, Setsu Goto, and began study at Juilliard School of Music

1986   July 26—Made historic performance at Tanglewood Music Festival

1987   Left Juilliard School of Music to become a professional violinist

1988   Named Japan's Best Artist of the Year

1991   Awarded New York State's Asian-American Heritage Month Award

1992   Made television appearance on the 1992 Winter Olympic Games telecast

INDEX

Asian American Heritage Month Award, 24
Aspen Summer Music Festival, 12, 13
awards, 24, 25
Bernstein, Leonard, 5, 8
Best Artist of the Year (award by Japanese government), 25
Boston Symphony Orchestra, 5
college, 28
Crystal Award, 25
DeLay, Dorothy, 11, 12, 13
Goto, Setsu (mother), 10, 11, 29

Japan, 24–25
Juilliard School of Music, 6, 11, 13, 20
Mehta, Zubin, 15–16
Midori Foundation, 30–31
music lessons, 11, 14, 15, 17, 20, 21
New Year's Eve concert, 16
New York City, 6, 11, 13, 14, 15
New York Philharmonic, 16
Osaka, Japan, 10, 14
performances, 5–9, 16, 17–19, 21–22, 24, 26–27
practice, 11, 17, 22, 29

prodigies, 25–26, 27
Professional Children's School, 21
recordings, 23
school, 14, 17, 21
"Serenade for Violin and String Orchestra," 5, 7
Tanglewood Music Festival, 5–8, 9, 20
television, 23
travel, 18, 29
Winter Olympic Games, 23
White House, 23
Zukerman, Pinchas, 13

ABOUT THE AUTHOR

Charnan Simon began her publishing career in the Children's Book Department of Little, Brown, and Company. After that she spent five busy years editing *Cricket Magazine*, where she read hundreds of great children's books and met many talented writers and artists. All of this was a tremendous help when she started writing her own books for young readers. Ms. Simon's most recent title for Childrens Press was *Henry the Navigator*. She lives in Chicago with her husband and two daughters, and she enjoys reading—and writing—history, biography, and fiction of all sorts.

04187-8

J
927
MID

Simon, Charnan
Midori